FISK UNIVERSITY LIBRARY

3.75

D1450753

MOROCCO

← A FIRST BOOK →

MOROCCO

BY BETTY CAVANNA

Illustrated with photographs

FRANKLIN WATTS, INC.
575 Lexington Avenue
New York, N.Y. 10022

MAPS BY WALTER HORTENS

COVER PHOTOGRAPH AND FRONTISPIECE: HUFFMAN—CUSHING.

SBN 531 00689-1

Library of Congress Catalog Card Number: 76-102369
© Copyright 1970 by Franklin Watts, Inc.
Printed in the United States of America

1 2 3 4 5

171663
c. 2

CONTENTS

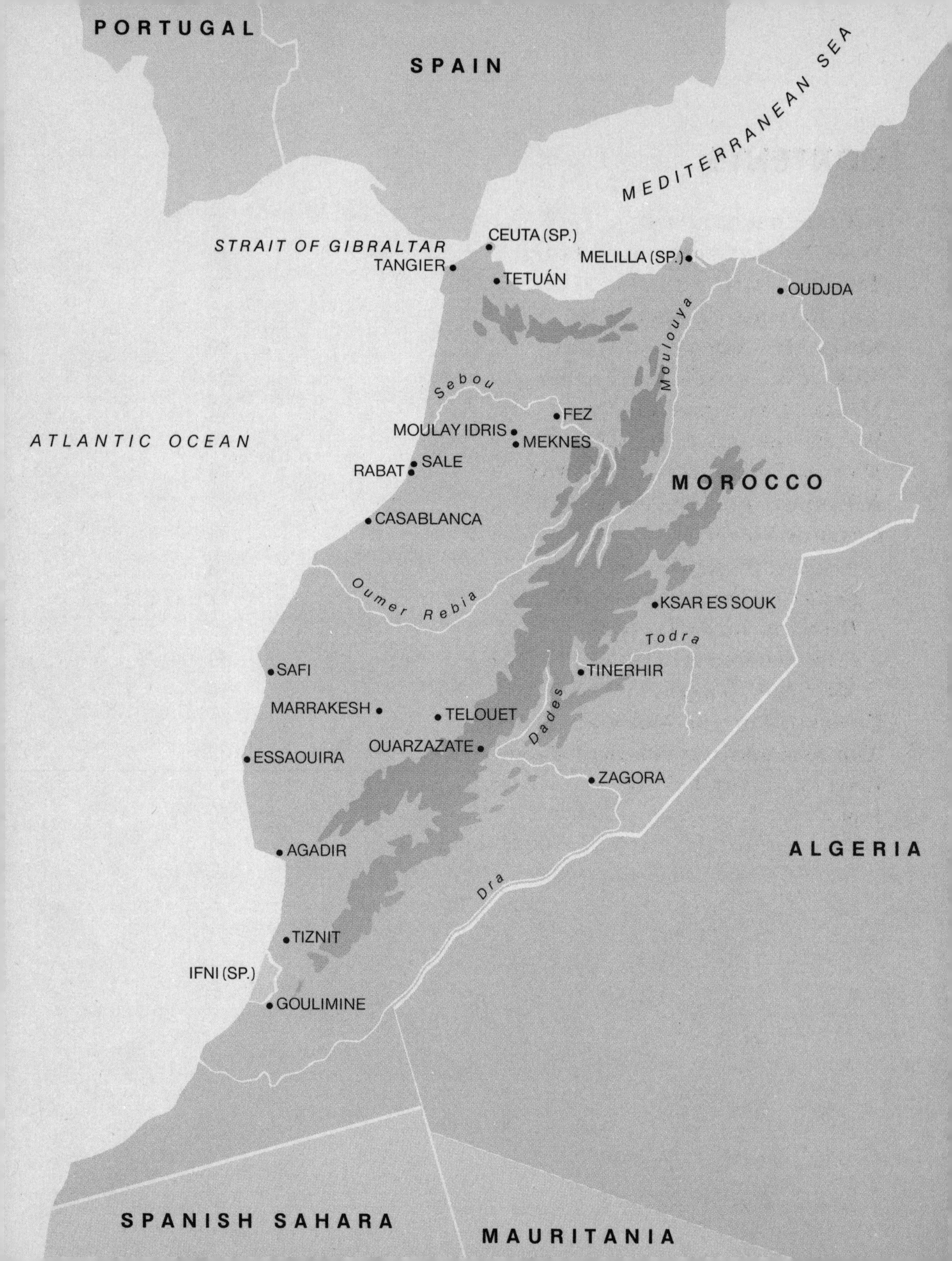

PORTUGAL

SPAIN

MEDITERRANEAN SEA

STRAIT OF GIBRALTAR
● CEUTA (SP.)
TANGIER ●
MELILLA (SP.) ●
● TETUÁN
● OUDJDA

Sebou

Moulouya

● FEZ
MOULAY IDRIS ●
● MEKNES

MOROCCO

RABAT ● ● SALE

ATLANTIC OCEAN

● CASABLANCA

Oumer Rebia

● KSAR ES SOUK

Todra

● SAFI

Dades

● TINERHIR

MARRAKESH ●

● TELOUET

OUARZAZATE ●

● ESSAOUIRA

● ZAGORA

● AGADIR

Dra

ALGERIA

● TIZNIT

IFNI (SP.)

● GOULIMINE

SPANISH SAHARA

MAURITANIA

A LAND OF CONTRASTS

Only a few miles south of Spain, across the narrow western entrance to the Mediterranean Sea called the Strait of Gibraltar, lies Morocco. It is a small country — only a little over 172,000 square miles in area — and is the westernmost of the Arab nations that range across the top of Africa through Egypt and into the Near East. On the east, Morocco is bordered by Algeria. Its other boundaries are: on the north, the Mediterranean Sea; on the west, the Atlantic Ocean; on the southwest, a stretch of sand and gravel known as the Spanish Sahara.

Morocco is varied in its geography and climate, although most of it is dry. Hundreds of miles of beautiful seacoasts rim arid hills and plains that rise to mountains so high that their peaks are often covered with snow, even in summer. Where water can be pumped from rivers and wells, irrigated farmlands are green with fields of barley, wheat, or corn, or with orchards of olives, almonds, oranges, or dates. Over much of the country, however, only a few inches of rain fall in an entire year. Dry, gravelly plains extend for hundreds of miles, and bleak, shifting sand dunes stretch for hundreds more, south and east, deep into Africa.

Along the Atlantic shoreline on the west are many sandy beaches separated by miles of cliff-lined shores. Only a few of the harbors are big enough to furnish protection for anything larger than fishing boats.

The Mediterranean seacoast on the north is backed by chains of low mountains called Er Rif, or the Rif, which run near the coast and parallel to it. As a consequence, the Mediterranean cliffs are rather isolated from the rest of the land.

Most of the more than fourteen million people of Morocco live north of three great mountain ranges that cross the country from northeast to southwest, south of the Rif. The Middle Atlas Mountains, rising near the Rif and running to the Atlantic coast, are rimmed with rich tablelands that furnish grazing for sheep and goats. The higher slopes of these mountains are covered with forests of oak, cedar, and pine. Here are found ski resorts — mountain villages built by Europeans during the French occupation of Morocco — which look much like villages in Switzerland. This region abounds in rocky springs, lakes and ponds, and streams well filled with trout. The mountain brooks feed several long rivers that flow across Morocco to the sea and furnish water to irrigate fields and gardens. Yet less than one acre in every forty of Moroccan land is cultivated. An equal area is covered with forest, but by far the most is pasture or arid desert.

The High Atlas mountain range, branching to the south from the Middle Atlas, has peaks that reach to heights of 14,000 feet. Roads running north and south cross these mountains through passes 7,000 feet high, but in winter these are sometimes filled with snow and so cannot be used. Because the northern slopes of the High Atlas catch moisture brought by storms from the Atlantic, they are densely covered with trees and scrub. On the south side, rainfall is so scanty that few plants can grow.

Between the High Atlas and the desert to the south and east lie the Anti-Atlas Mountains. The road across the southern foothills of these mountains travels beside the beds of several rivers that flow into the Sahara Desert. This great desert stretches far beyond the boundaries of Morocco, toward Central Africa.

Near the town of Tiznit on the edge of the Sahara is a sign that reads: 32 DAYS BY CAMEL TRAIN TO TIMBUKTU. This city, where several ancient caravan routes across the desert converge, lies far

At Tinerhir oasis, where water is plentiful, date palms and other plants flourish. (Huffman—Cushing)

to the south and east, near the Niger River. Timbuctoo, as it is sometimes spelled, is often used as a symbol of the place that is farthest away in the whole world.

A camel train moves away from an oasis, into the desert. (Huffman—Cushing)

FROM ANCIENT TO MODERN TIMES

Morocco has existed as a modern nation only since 1956. Yet the country has been inhabited for hundreds of centuries. The years of its long history have been filled with the comings and goings of many different groups of people, and with terrible wars. From time to time, pirates have landed on both coasts, the Atlantic and the Mediterranean, and raiding tribes from Algeria and the Sahara have come frequently to plunder. The people who owned the land belonged to hundreds of tribes that fought each other for pastures and water. There was no central government with an army to keep order and peace, except during times when one warlord was strong enough to subdue all the others.

Several thousand years before Christ, the Phoenicians and other people who traveled the Mediterranean Sea used harbors in Morocco as stopping points. In early historical times, from about 1200 B.C., Morocco was the area farthest west in the empire of Carthage. About one thousand years later, with the fall of Carthage in 146 B.C., the Romans became the rulers. Today, old Roman ruins may still be seen in parts of Morocco.

With the decline of the Roman Empire, the country was overrun from across the Strait of Gibraltar by a horde of barbarians called the Vandals. Reconquered once more by Romans, it was invaded by Arabs from the east around A.D. 700. They brought their ancient culture, their written language, and the Moslem religion, all of which have been important in the development of modern Morocco.

In 788, the Berber tribes who had lived in the country since early times were united under Idris I. His son, Idris II, founded the city of Fez as the capital in 808.

About A.D. 800, North African people called Moors, of mixed Berber and Arab descent, overran the Iberian Peninsula occupied

A sculpture from the ruins of the ancient Roman city of Volubilis, in Morocco. (Huffman—Cushing)

by Spain and Portugal, and held much of it for several hundred years.

Morocco's position in the northwest corner of Africa, close to Europe, has made it a thoroughfare for people coming from farther east, and a steppingstone to the land across the Strait of Gibraltar. The first great Moroccan empire was that of the Almoravides, founded in the eleventh century. It extended over part of North Africa and up into Spain.

For several centuries a series of dynasties ruled in Morocco. Gradually the Moors were driven out of Spain, and by the fourteenth century many of them had settled in North Africa. Over the years, Morocco lost outlying territory, and Spain and Portugal even invaded and held several of its ports.

From the sixteenth to the nineteenth centuries, Morocco, with other countries in northwest Africa, was the base for pirates who plundered ships sailing the Mediterranean Sea and held their crews for slavery or ransom. The piracy was stopped only with the conquest of Algeria by France in 1830.

When warring tribes caused an increase of revolt and lawlessness in Morocco in the early 1900's, France undertook to oversee the country, and thereafter both Spain and France had interests in Morocco. Further turmoil resulted in a dispute among France, Spain, and Germany, and led to a treaty establishing what amounted to a French protectorate of Morocco. Later agreements with Spain set up a Spanish zone in the northern part of the country.

Under Marshal Lyautey, the French resident-general, a start was made at pacifying the French protectorate, but in the Spanish section — the Rif — Berber guerrillas led by Abd-el-Krim forced the Spanish into the coastal towns. When Abd-el Krim invaded the French territory he was defeated and exiled.

Acting through sultans who did what they were told, and exiling any rulers who were disobedient, the French ruled Morocco for forty-four years after 1912. But although the Europeans built good roads and harbors in the country and managed to stimulate trade and raise somewhat the standard of living of the people, the Moroccans wanted liberty. A nationalist movement eventually gained strength, and in 1956, France granted Morocco her independence. The displaced sultan was recalled from his exile in Madagascar and became King Mohammed V of Morocco.

He died in 1961, and his eldest son became King Hassan II. This ruler is chief of state, head of the government, leader of the nation's principal religion, and commander in chief of the army — a powerful man. Educated and modern in his viewpoints, Hassan has tried to use his power wisely.

He has been faced with a multitude of problems. Morocco is a

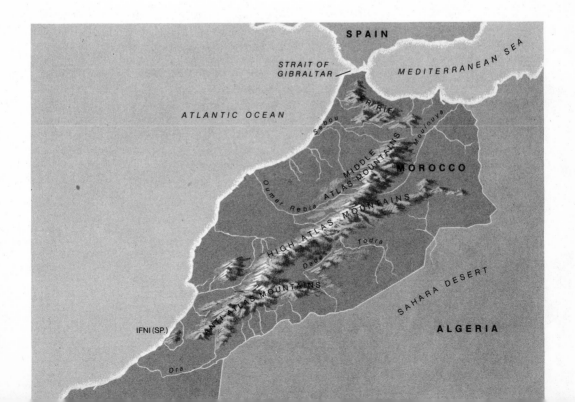

country that is divided geographically into many different sections; its people are from a variety of backgrounds; they speak numerous languages and dialects; they have differing outlooks; and many of them have strong tribal loyalties. Bringing such varied groups together to act and feel as a nation is difficult.

King Hassan has set the goal of democracy. The country has an elected Parliament. Fortunately, the tribal groups have had experience in local government and have long conducted their affairs in a democratic way. But local loyalties are often stronger than national ones. Tradition is very strong, and many people in the rural areas do not take easily to new ideas.

Much needs to be done to improve education, health, and the general welfare. The population is growing faster than industry or the food supply, and many Moroccans are unemployed and live in great poverty. Mindful of the people's strong feeling for tradition, King Hassan, though forward-looking, must show respect for the old ways, too. Even so, Morocco is gradually developing into a modern nation.

This Moroccan is a Berber. (Bertrand, Marrakesh)

THE BERBERS AND THE ARABS

Although the native people of Morocco all speak some form of Arabic, there are still two basic racial groups: the Berbers and the Arabs. These have intermingled over the thirteen centuries that they have occupied the country together, but if you ask a Moroccan about his ancestry, he is likely to reply with quiet pride, "I am a Berber," or "I am an Arab."

The Berbers are a white people who have inhabited much of North Africa for more than three thousand years. The dialects spoken by the modern Berbers of Morocco contain many words that came from an ancient language spoken in Libya, a country to the east, toward Egypt. Although some of the Berbers had a written language, it was not widely used, and it was not until the Arabs brought Arabic writing that Berbers from one part of Morocco found it possible to understand those from another part. They still pronounce many words differently and often use different words for the same thing.

In the very distant past, when three great tribes of Berbers overran Morocco, one tribe settled in fairly flat country just inland from the Atlantic coast in the northwest, where rivers provided plenty of water. The descendants of these people became farmers. Another clan moved into the highlands of the Atlas Mountains and beyond, and became herdsmen, raising sheep and goats for meat, wool, and leather. Many of these people eventually became fine horsemen. A third group conquered parts of the Sahara and became camel-riding nomads.

The ancestors of the dark-haired, dark-eyed Arabs came in the eighth century A.D., having worked their way westward from Arabia over the centuries. Because the written language that the Arabs

15

brought to Morocco provided a way of communication for the whole country, it was soon adopted. The Arabs also brought their new religion and an ancient way of living that appealed to the Berbers.

Although poorer Moroccans still usually have little education, the Arabs have always had great respect for learning and have founded many schools and universities. Many highly educated Berbers and Arabs are professional men in the cities, and others work in the growing industrial plants. Those Arabs with less education are often craftsmen, working leather, copper, or iron, or dyeing wool with bright colors and weaving it into cloth and rugs. The people who live in the desert are usually nomad herdsmen. Most of their work is done by the women, who pitch the tents at a new campsite, cook, sew, weave, gather feed to supplement that picked up by the flocks, and even at times watch the herds.

In addition to the Berbers, the Arabs, and many people of Jewish descent, Morocco has large numbers of black-skinned people, especially in the south. The ancestors of these people came north across the desert from the Sudan or from other parts of Africa. Gradually they are intermarrying with the white races of northern Africa.

Two Moroccan children from the northern edge of the Sahara Desert. (George R. Harrison)

THE RELIGION OF MOHAMMED

Most Moroccans are very religious. The majority are Moslems, or followers of the prophet Mohammed, who lived in Arabia about fourteen hundred years ago. It is said that as he meditated alone there came to him visions of one all-powerful God, whom Moslems call Allah. Mohammed's visions and teachings are included in a sacred book, the Koran, which is the Bible of the Moslems. The Moslem religion is the prevailing one in most Arab lands.

The name of the prophet is sometimes spelled Mahomet, and even in other ways such as M'h'm't. These variations occur because vowel sounds are often not written out in the Arabic language; presumably the reader knows how to fill in the blanks where vowels would be. As a result, an "o" sound may gradually be changed to an "a" sound in one Arabic-speaking land, and not in another.

A basic statement of the Moslem religion is, "There is no god but Allah, and Mohammed is his prophet." When talking together, Moslems frequently say, "If it be the will of Allah," or "May Allah provide." The name of Allah is used in most greetings and partings, just as people in English-speaking countries say "Good-bye," a short form of "God be with you."

Unlike most other religious groups, the Moslems have no ministers or priests, although they do have religious teachers. But every good Moslem prays five times a day. In a town or city he will be reminded to do so by a man called a *muezzin* (mu-EZ-n), who summons the faithful to prayer from a tall tower, or minaret (min-a-RET). In the old days the *muezzin* climbed to his lofty perch by a ladder or a narrow staircase. Today he is more likely to stay down below and call into a microphone while loudspeakers at the top

One of the most famous minarets in Morocco, the Koutoubiya, in Marrakesh. (George R. Harrison)

of the minaret make his voice heard for many blocks around.

From dawn to long after sunset there are set times for Moslems to pray. The devout then kneel facing Mecca, the holy city far to the east in Saudi Arabia, where the religion was founded. Before entering a mosque (MOSK), or temple, a Moslem washes his face, his hands and arms, and sometimes his feet, so that he will feel purified while praying.

There are many beautiful mosques in Morocco. Some of these

are considered so sacred that infidels — people who are not Moslems — are not permitted to enter them.

Because one of the teachings of the Koran is that no living creature shall be depicted, paintings or statues of people or animals are never used in Moslem countries. Instead, artists carve wood and stone into beautiful designs. Often they make a great archway look as if it were covered with lace, so delicate and intricate are the traceries on it.

Instead of reserving Sunday as a day of rest and religious activity, as is done in Christian countries, Moslems observe Friday as a holy day. As a result, in many Moroccan cities the banks and some of the stores remain closed for a three-day weekend, shutting down on Friday out of respect for the Moslem people, on Saturday for the Jewish people, and on Sunday for the Christian people.

The Moslem calendar is different from the one commonly used in the Western world. The Moslem year is only 354 days long instead of 365, and the months have alternately thirty or twenty-nine days each. Instead of numbering the years from the birth of Christ, the Moslems start counting from the time Mohammed went from Mecca to Medina. This journey, called the Hegira (hej-EYE-ra), took place in A.D. 622.

The ninth month in the Moslem year is a holy one called Ramadan (ra-ma-DAHN). During this entire month, Moslems — who are forbidden to drink alcohol at any time — do not eat, smoke, or drink even water between sunrise and sunset. A long, hot day may make this practice a real sacrifice.

Many religious men in Morocco spend their entire lives studying and interpreting the writings of the prophet Mohammed, and students in the schools and universities devote much time to religious studies.

Two Moroccan men in *jellabas* discuss politics in the marketplace. (George R. Harrison)

ROBED MEN AND VEILED WOMEN

Although many Moroccan businessmen in the cities wear European clothes, most of the native people dress in the robes so common in African desert countries. The Sahara, which is the largest desert on earth, covers about one fourth of the entire African continent, and a full third of Morocco lies in and near it. The desert air may reach a temperature of 120°F. during the day. But soon after the sun sets, the air may cool off by as much as fifty degrees, and feel chilly in comparison with the earlier heat. Clothing therefore is planned to keep its wearers as cool as possible in the daytime and warm at night.

The garment most suitable for wear in extreme heat and moderate cold is a loose, floppy robe, preferably made of wool. As the wearer moves his arms and legs the cloth acts as a bellows, first pulling air in and circulating it around his body, then pumping it out again laden with the cooling moisture of perspiration. In the evening the robe can be held close around the wearer, so preventing warm air from escaping.

In Morocco such a robe is called a *jellaba* (juh-LAH-buh), sometimes written *djellaba,* while in Egypt, to the east, it is called a *galabeah* (gal-ah-BAY-yuh). These are different ways of spelling the same Arabic word, pronounced somewhat differently in lands so far apart.

Although many *jellabas* are made of cotton, wool holds heat better while actually helping moisture to escape. Wool may be white, gray, black, or brown, depending on the sheep from which it is sheared. *Jellabas* for men are usually handwoven in these natural colors. But white wool can be dyed, and the robes of women are ordinarily dyed gray. Sometimes *jellabas* are striped in various colors, to indicate the region or village from which their wearers come.

In Morocco the sun is often so hot that people must keep their heads covered when out of doors. And in the desert, protection is needed against sand blown by the wind. The best defense against both sun and sand is a loose hood called a burnoose, either fastened to the robe, or flowing down over the neck, with a heavy veil to cover most of the face.

A turban, a long piece of cloth wound around the head and tucked in at the ends, is another common headdress. A turban allows perspiration to escape through its folds, and also makes a soft cushion for carrying things on the head. Countrypeople bear

Two Riffian peasant women, wearing straw hats over their hoods. (Huffman—Cushing)

all sorts of loads — even lumber and ladders — in this way, and every young girl learns to balance a jug of water or a basketful of laundry without a steadying hand.

Seen less often today than the hood or the turban, but worn sometimes by merchants or guides or by men with European clothes, is a flat-topped conical red hat with a tassel. Outsiders call it a fez. In Morocco it is known as a *tarboosh* (tar-BOOSH). More common than the *tarboosh* is a small knitted skullcap, often worn by laborers.

Moroccan women usually wear a flowing hood. Although some women now appear in public with their faces uncovered, most still wear a veil. In parts of northern Morocco, women wear broad, flat straw hats to shield their faces from the sun.

There is not much variation in shoes, for almost everyone wears *babouches* (ba-BOOSH-ez), soft Moroccan leather slippers that seem to stay on even though they are all front and no back.

22

MOROCCAN COOKING AND EATING

Moroccans are fond of spicy flavors and odors. They may season a dish of turnips with bitter orange; or a piece of fish with garlic, lemon, and a spice called cumin (KUM-in). They also like fruit, and raise apricots, cherries, pears, plums, mulberries, figs, pomegranates, yellow melons, watermelons, and grapes tinged by the desert sun. When winter comes and these fruits are not available, Moroccans eat oranges, raisins, dried figs, and dates.

A Moroccan mother and her child. (Zeitsma—Cushing)

A laborer taking his lunch to work is likely to eat only a part of a loaf of bread, and a dozen or two ripe olives. But Moroccans are fond of lengthy banquets that have many courses. Among their favorite dishes are roast mutton and goats' meat, which may be cut into chunks, threaded onto a sharp metal rod along with peppers and tomatoes, and roasted over hot coals. Another favorite is couscous (KOOS-koos). This dish is made of semolina, coarse-ground wheat, boiled into mush; to it other ingredients such as olives, raisins, and chick-peas are added. Moroccans also like spicy chunks of chicken in a sort of stew that contains onions, almonds, and honey.

A favorite dish is pigeon pie, deliciously sweetened with sugar and cinnamon and covered with a pastry made of countless thin layers of flaky crust. Since it is a Moroccan custom to use the fingers in eating, instead of forks, this pie is easier to manage than the stew is.

At a formal meal the diners sit on sofas around a low table. Each person uses three fingers of his right hand to take from a common dish the morsels he wants to eat. His hand is washed at the table before the meal starts, when a waiter, or a woman of the family, brings in towels and a kettle of warm water. The diner holds his eating hand above a basin while water is poured over it. At the end of the meal the hand is again washed and dried.

It is fascinating to watch a Moroccan reach into a big bowl of couscous, pick up with his fingers an olive, a raisin, or some similar solid lump, twirl it around in the mush to cover it with semolina, and put it in his mouth. In the cruel days of long ago a thief was sometimes sentenced to have his right hand cut off. Besides branding him for life, this punishment kept him from ever again eating with other people, for the right hand is the clean hand, which every-

Women in a mountain village prepare food for a community feast. They quickly veiled their faces when the cameraman appeared. (George R. Harrison)

one uses for eating. The left hand, reserved for mundane duties such as scratching, could never be dipped into the communal dish of stew or couscous.

The most commonly used drink in Morocco is a very sweet green tea flavored with mint, which is taken with meals and often in between. Even when it is drunk hot, this beverage is refreshing and cooling. To make it, a handful of fresh green mint is crushed into tea of the ordinary sort, and hot water is poured over it. A great deal of mint is grown in Morocco just for use in tea, and bundles of mint can be bought in the markets.

Moroccans have been drinking mint tea for only a little over a century. When the Black Sea was blockaded in 1854 at the time of the Crimean War, British merchants were unable to sell their tea in the usual markets. So they shipped it to new places, Tangier (tan-JEER) and Mogador (mog-a-DOR) among them. The Moroccans liked the unfamiliar beverage, and tried adding crushed mint to it. Soon they had invented a new national drink.

Each part of the world has its typical foods that have starch, important for furnishing body energy. Ireland has potatoes; Italy has macaroni and spaghetti made from wheat flour; Japan and parts of China have rice. In Morocco, starch comes from wheat, maize, and barley, used either as cereal or as flour baked into bread. Bread can be bought in the *souks* (SOOKS) or marketplaces, but is usually made at home. A housewife in a village ordinarily kneads and shapes her own loaves. Then she sends them, balanced on a tray on the head of one of her children, to a community oven where all the neighborhood's flat loaves are baked at one time.

In the country districts most cooking is done on clay braziers or a stove covered with tiles, in dark and primitive kitchens, or perhaps outdoors. The common cooking fuel is charcoal, made in mountain districts by setting fire to a great pile of branches and covering it with earth when it is half burned. But charcoal is best made in large pits or clay ovens whose air supply is cut off halfway through the process. When the charcoal is cool, it is piled up, put into sacks, and sent to market for sale.

MARKET DAY IN THE COUNTRY

Almost three-quarters of the people in Morocco live in country villages, on farms, or in tents while they tend their flocks. The villages have few stores, and most supplies are bought in *souks* on market days, which occur once a week. Then the farmers for miles around come on foot, in buses, or on their burros or bicycles, to a central market held in a large enclosure. There the farmers sell their produce and buy the goods they need. Nearby, if they wish, they can pitch their tents, tether their burros, or park their carts and bicycles.

The names of many Moroccan villages indicate the day on which the weekly market is held. Thus Souk-el-Khemis is the Arabic name for Market on Thursday. Other villages are called Souk-el-Tleta (Market on Tuesday), Souk-el-Arba (Market on Wednesday), or Souk-el-Sebt (Market on Saturday).

Besides giving an opportunity for shopping, the weekly market day is a social occasion for visiting with friends and catching up on the news. This day looms large in the lives of countrypeople, and takes the place of motion pictures, church fairs, and other entertainment. But its main purpose is to collect the week's supplies and to sell or barter produce.

A market is a busy place. Here one farmer carries a cluster of live chickens with their feet tied together and their heads hanging down. Another farmer holds a basket of eggs, which he will exchange two or three at a time for a few tomatoes, some red peppers, or some dry-looking ears of corn. A bearded man sits behind a basket of homemade soap, which he has cooked up by boiling ashes from his kitchen fire with fat cut from meat.

At one spot stands a great pile of yellow melons, fine for satisfying both thirst and hunger in a hot, dry climate. Next to the melons a wizened Arab squats beside a small charcoal fire burning in a brazier. He is cooking sizzling chunks of mutton on skewers; he will sell the meat at lunchtime. Nearby stands a water carrier, ready to exchange a cupful of water from his goatskin for a very small coin.

The weekly market at Chauen, a town in the Rif. (George R. Harrison)

People arrive at market by various means of transportation, modern and ancient. (Huffman—Cushing)

The money used in Morocco is based on that of France, which occupied the country for a long time. Instead of dollars, dirhams (dir-HAMZ) are used. The symbol for this unit of money is written dh. A dirham is composed of 100 francs, and is now worth about 20 cents in United States money. But in many transactions no money is used. Instead, a chicken is traded for a length of cloth, or three eggs for half a dozen oranges.

A river in central Morocco. (George R. Harrison)

WATER, THE GREAT PROBLEM

Nineteen out of twenty acres of Moroccan farmland are so dry, except after the occasional rains from October to May, that only skimpy tufts of grass can grow on them. Where the land can be irrigated it is often very fertile and will produce fine fruits and vegetables. But only near the rivers is there usually enough water for irrigation. Then the problem is to find power to pump the water so that it can be raised to flow across the higher fields. Electric power is scarce in Morocco except near the mountains, where streams can be dammed. Power can then be generated by hydro-electric stations.

Morocco depends mainly on its yearly rainfall; if rain is scarce, crops and food are scarce. More dams would help conserve water flowing from the mountains. Part of the national five-year plan is the building of forty new dams and the eventual irrigation of 2½ million additional acres. Some of the dams are already being constructed. When they are completed, Morocco will have made great strides in solving the water problem.

But despite advances, many of the Moroccan farms and villages remain in a primitive state. Sometimes a river itself is used to raise water to the level of the land by means of a large wooden waterwheel of ancient design. The wheel has buckets fastened to its rim, and as it is turned by the stream the water in these receptacles is lifted and dumped into wooden flumes that channel it to irrigation ditches.

A wooden waterwheel, turned by the current of a Moroccan stream, carries water up to a wooden irrigation flume by means of buckets on its rim. (George R. Harrison)

Where there are wells, the water is often pumped by patient camels that walk in a circle, turning wooden gears that drive the pumping machinery.

South of the Atlas ranges, water becomes even more scarce than in the hilly districts, until in the Sahara it is found only in oases. Most of this desert is gravelly; shifting sand dunes cover only one tenth of its area. In an oasis, water may lie in small pools or may be so close to the surface that wells can be dug to reach it. In some parts of the desert the oases are hundreds of miles apart. The tall date palms that may surround a water hole are a welcome sight to a traveler with a thirsty camel caravan.

Usually the water in an oasis comes from an underground river that may flow far beneath the sand and gravel for hundreds of miles. From the Atlas Mountains several large rivers reach into the desert, among them the Todra, the Dades, and the Dra. Water from snow melting in the mountains runs in these rivers for long distances, but eventually vanishes into the sand. There it may continue to flow as far again underground. Only when the heaviest snows are melting in the mountains is there enough water to reach the mouth of the Dra at the Atlantic Ocean.

Before the desert is reached, but where the hills already look as dry as the mountains of the moon, the river valleys form great oases filled with cultivated fields. Beside the riverbeds stretch long chains of villages called *ksour* (k-SOOR). (One such village is called a *ksar*.) At intervals there are citadels or fortresses called *casbahs* (KAZ-bahz), which were built for defense against the nomad bands that frequently attacked the villages in the past.

Almost continuous rows of villages stretch with their forts for hundreds of miles along roads that parallel the riverbeds leading into the desert. The name "road of the *casbahs*" is often given

A river flowing into the Sahara Desert from the Atlas Mountains makes a long oasis that is bordered by farms and villages. (George R. Harrison)

these routes. They extend almost continuously between Ouarzazate and Tinerhir, and between Ouarzazate and Zagora, on the northern rim of the desert.

The villages along the desert trade routes are less important now than they were when caravans passed through frequently. In those days, desert raiders sometimes came and did a great deal of damage. Now caravans of desert people come in peace to the vil-

Tafilalet, a casbah village in the valley of the Ziz, a stream that flows into the desert. (Huffman—Cushing)

lages to trade their young camels and donkeys, their dates, and their handicrafts for sugar, salt, and grain.

Because many of the people who live in the *ksour* today have difficulty in supporting their families by farming, the women weave cloth and rugs while the men tan hides and use the leather to make saddles and slippers.

In the cities of Morocco, water carriers are among the most picturesque people to be seen. Since there is little plumbing in a *medina* (me-DEE-na), or native quarter, and water is piped to only a few locations, water carriers are important. Each one carries a goatskin water bag — a goat's hide that has been stripped from an animal killed for its meat. The stripping is carefully done, so that there will be few holes in the skin. Those that exist are sewed up and coated with wax, and the whole skin is thoroughly cleaned.

Then straps are fastened to it so that it can be carried on a man's back. A small spigot is tied and waxed into one of the holes left at the end of a leg. The resulting bag holds several gallons of water, which is doled out in a dozen or so brass cups held on straps fastened to the water carrier's harness.

Slowly he walks around in the hot sun, looking for thirsty people who will pay him a small coin for a cup of water. He calls *"Ma! Ma!"* — the Arabic for "Water! Water!" Since the cups are only scantily rinsed after each use, drinking from them is not very sanitary.

In cities where there are many tourists, the water carrier, hoping to attract attention, often wears a flat hat decorated with tassels, pompons, bells, and colored beads. He probably earns as much money posing to have his picture taken as he does selling water.

A water carrier of Fez. He rings his bell to attract thirsty customers. (George R. Harrison)

MAKING THINGS IN THE OLD WAY

Morocco is only now emerging into the modern world. There are increasing numbers of factories containing machines operated by electric power, but many kinds of goods that cannot be made easily by hand must still be imported. Imports include such factory products as bicycles, buses, and cars. Raw materials that the country does not produce — such as gasoline and fuel oil — and foods that cannot be raised — such as sugar and tea — also must be bought abroad. To help pay for these goods, money must be earned by selling local products abroad.

Among the principal exports are minerals from Moroccan mines — manganese, zinc, iron, cobalt, lead, salt, and phosphates; fruits such as oranges, olives, and dates; palm and grass fibers; cork; and canned fish. Safi (SAF-fee), on the Atlantic coast, is one of the most active sardine fishing ports in the world, and large canneries are operated there. In addition, the country exports the handicrafts made, often with great artistic skill, by its artisans. Increasingly, modern machines are being used, but many craftsmen still work in the age-old way of their ancestors.

In a *souk* in Marrakesh (ma-RAH-kesh) sits a young boy who turns a primitive lathe by means of a bow whose string is wrapped around the spindle of the lathe. The piece of wood fastened to the spindle turns when the bow is sawed back and forth. Since the boy uses one of his hands to operate the bow, he lets one of his big toes help the other hand support the tool with which he cuts away the wood as it turns. He is shaping a round ferrule that will be used in making the back of a chair.

Nearby, in another *souk,* a boy is dipping a finger into a jar of blue pigment and painting a design on a piece of glazed clay pot-

The government, with the help of experts from other countries, is trying to introduce modern methods of manufacturing leather goods. Here apprentices work at shoemaking. (United Nations)

This boy has no motor to turn his lathe. He spins the wood with a string bow held in his right hand and uses his left hand and a toe to guide his cutting tool. (George R. Harrison)

Skeins of wool, after they are dyed, are hung to dry on long poles over the street. (George R. Harrison)

tery. When he finishes decorating the piece of pottery, it will be baked in a hot oven so that the pigment will be burned into the glaze.

Certain Moroccan towns are celebrated for their skilled cabinet-makers, who fashion tables, desks, and other furniture inlaid with thin pieces of wood of various colors. In other towns there are gold-smiths and silversmiths who make jewelry that is sold around the world.

Expensive books in special editions are often bound in Moroccan leather. After the skins of sheep and goats have been tanned, they are dyed red, brown, purple, yellow, green, or blue, and are then pressed with dull tools that emboss designs on the soft leather. Sometimes the impressions are later filled with gold leaf. Moroccan leather is also fashioned into handbags, hassocks, and the slippers called *babouches*.

A great deal of wool is produced in Morocco. It is spun into fluffy threads and then dipped into large pottery vats filled with dyes. The wool, dripping with dye, is festooned over long poles to dry, and then is sold in the *souks* to weavers.

Rugs are in great demand for the floors of tents and houses and as prayer rugs, as well as for shipment abroad. Such rugs are usually woven by hand. Long rows of warp threads are stretched tight on wooden looms, and the woof threads are passed between them, as in the weaving of an ordinary piece of cloth. Then thousands of woolen strands are knotted into loops around both sets of threads, and are packed as closely together as possible. When the entire rug has been knotted, the tops of the loops are trimmed off evenly. Short tufts of thread are left standing straight up to form the soft pile of the rug, which can resist wear for many years. By properly selecting woolen strands of various colors, weavers can make rugs with beautiful designs.

The Moroccans weave matting by laying reeds close together and binding them tightly between stretched warp threads. Weavers also make baskets — some of them taller than a man and capable of holding more than a hundred pounds of grain. Double baskets — two baskets joined together — are woven to throw over the backs of donkeys and camels. One basket hangs on each side of the animal, and the load on one side can be balanced against that on the other.

In the *souks,* tailors do exquisite needlework, embroidering silken clothing with colored threads or strands of silver and gold. Often, when several colors are being used to make an intricate design, a tailor will handle half a dozen threads at once. So that they will not become tangled, he has a little boy hold them taut and feed them out slowly through the spaces between his toes.

Cooking pots, pots for plants, and others for carrying water are made by shaping damp clay on a flat potter's wheel, where the clay is formed and smoothed as it spins around. After the article has been dried, dipped in glaze, and decorated, it is put with hundreds of other clay objects into a large kiln, or oven. Here the clay is baked for hours at a high temperature until it has a hard, shiny surface.

Another ancient product of Morocco is rosewater, a perfume that smells much like fresh roses. Near the edge of the desert, acres of rose bushes grow in fields in oases that stretch for nearly a hundred miles. When the roses bloom, their petals are gathered in large baskets and are carried to a still to be boiled in water. In the still the vapor that boils off is condensed into an oil called attar of roses, which is especially prized in Morocco for perfuming the water with which a diner's eating hand is rinsed before and after a meal.

A FANTASIA IN A HOLY CITY

One of the favorite pastimes of Moroccans is watching a fantasia, a wild display of horsemanship. This is a survival of the days when the members of various tribes fought one another on horseback. A fantasia is often held in connection with a religious festival. Probably the most famous are the fantasias held once a year in the holy city of Moulay Idris (moo-LAY ee-DREES).

When the holy days approach, people from miles around come to Moulay Idris and camp in tents on the hills about the city. Moulay Idris is revered because, centuries ago, a man from Arabia who claimed to be a relative of the prophet Mohammed arrived there and was welcomed by members of a Berber tribe, to whom he brought the Moslem religion. Today only Moslems are permitted to live in the city. While visitors of all faiths may watch the fantasia and other ceremonies that are held outdoors, they are not allowed to enter mosques and other religious buildings.

The Moroccans have always been able breeders of horses, intermingling famous Arab and Berber strains to produce beautifully trained animals of great speed and stamina. In Meknès (mek-NESS) the king of Morocco now has large stables devoted to the improvement of the bloodlines of Moroccan horses. There the ancestry of each of his more than four hundred stallions has been carefully recorded.

A fantasia consists of a series of charges down an open field several hundred yards long, by horsemen who are usually dressed in white robes and turbans. Their guns and saddles are richly ornamented, and they wear jeweled daggers at their belts. Each village sends its own group of riders, and each group tries to top the others in its skill and the training of its horses.

Two riders, on horses wearing ornate decorations, prepare to take part in a fantasia. (George R. Harrison)

The field is entirely surrounded by standing people who watch the charging animals. The spectators have come wearing their finest clothes, and the gaily colored shawls and dresses of the women look like a flower garden on a spring day.

At a signal from their leader, a group of from six to ten horsemen go galloping down the field as fast as their mounts can travel. About two-thirds of the way to the end, at another signal, all the riders raise their muskets, stand up in their stirrups, and shoot off their guns in a tremendous salvo. Their ancient ornamented weapons are loaded with a kind of powder that makes a great noise and clouds of smoke. The riders are so busy standing up, keeping their balance, and firing their guns that they have no time to guide their horses, which have been trained to continue their furious gallop without flinching at the noise and smoke. At the far end of the field all the horsemen stop together within a few feet, and the horses turn around and trot slowly back to where they started, while the dust and smoke drift away.

It is easy to see how a fantasia originated in the galloping charge of actual warriors as they attempted to terrify an opposing army by the fury of their noisy attack, and to cause it to break and run.

A group of riders fire their guns before the fantasia begins, to show that their horses will not flinch at the smoke and noise. (George R. Harrison)

CITIES OF MOROCCO

Morocco contains five large cities; most of them are many centuries old. The country owes much of its charm to their palaces and mosques, their towering minarets, and their beautiful arches, all decorated in the Moorish manner with delicate carvings in stone and wood.

Although most Moroccan cities have broad avenues lined with modern stores and houses, the busiest part of each city is its *medina* (me-DEE-na), the ancient native section. The *medina* is usually surrounded by a thick wall higher than a house, built centuries ago of stones and clay to keep out bands of robbers.

Most of the narrow alleys of the *medina* are lined with *souks* — markets filled with tiny stalls where, in the ancient way of Eastern peoples, merchants haggle over the prices with their customers. In one alley, several *souks* may have shelves stacked with shoes and other goods of soft Moroccan leather. The walls of another group of *souks* may be hung with trays of hammered brass and copper, long-spouted teapots, and ornamented guns and daggers. In front of some *souks* will stand big baskets heaped with grains and spices, with crude brown soap, or with broken cakes of dirty-looking salt. At the joining of two alleys there is likely to be a pushcart filled with pomegranates, a fruit whose purple juice — in a warm land on a hot day — tastes like nectar.

A shopper pushing his way through the crowded marketplace is likely to be jostled by burros bearing bales of merchandise and ridden by men who call *"Balek! Balek!"* — "Make way! Make way!" Or the shopper may be bumped by a goat bleating as it is tugged unwillingly to market. The scene looks like one in Biblical lands and times.

The *medina,* or old section, of a Moroccan city. This street is lined with
market stalls. (George R. Harrison)

Tangier, Where West Meets East

The Moroccan city best known to Europeans is Tangier, which
gave its name to the sweet, loose-skinned oranges known as tan-
gerines. Tangier is built on hills around a beautiful harbor from
which ferries cross the Strait of Gibraltar to the coastal cities of
Spain. Ocean liners come to Tangier, a favorite spot for tourists
visiting countries around the Mediterranean Sea. The number of
ships passing by the city in a year is said to be more than sixty
thousand.

The climate of Tangier is balmy, and near its white, sandy beach, which is fully three miles long, camels graze. Because it is more exposed to the rest of the world than other Moroccan cities and is a convenient port, Tangier has changed hands many times. The ancient Phoenicians used it as a harbor when they piloted their boats from one end of the Mediterranean to the other. More than sixteen hundred years ago the Romans made it a stopping place on their journeys to and from the British Isles.

Despite the strong European flavor of its hotels and shops, much of Tangier is typical of the Moroccan cities farther to the south. Its *medina, souks,* and *casbah* are like those in Rabat (ra-BAHT),

Ships in the harbor of Tangier. Gibraltar can be seen dimly in the far distance. (George R. Harrison)

Fez, or Marrakesh. Typically African is the donkey-parking lot, a field near the farmers' market, where hundreds of burros stand patiently all day long while the countrypeople who own them do their trading in live chickens, mutton and goats' meat, tomatoes, onions, peppers, meal, sugar, and salt.

Fez, a City from the Arabian Nights

The most colorful of ancient Moroccan cities is Fez, often called the cultural center of the country. Fez has two parts, separated by a muddy but life-giving river. The older city, founded almost twelve hundred years ago, is surrounded by the usual high walls. The newer part is a modern European section built by the French about forty years ago.

Fez is a vital commercial center — a market for the products brought by caravan from the desert. It is also a distributing point for fruits grown in the surrounding regions. Among its manufactures are textiles, soap, leather, rugs, and flour.

A constant procession streams through huge gates in the walls of the old city — a procession of robed Berbers and Arabs in turbans and burnooses; veiled women; hordes of ragged children; flocks of sheep and goats; pack animals laden with bales of goods; and an occasional water cart. Inside some of the gates lie parks, green gardens, and cooling streams, while other gates open onto a maze of narrow alleys that thread the *medina.* To go through these alleys, a person must either walk, or travel on the back of a small donkey, as the streets are too narrow for a car to enter.

Although the river that flows through Fez keeps the gardens lush, water is not piped throughout the *medina,* but only to certain places fitted with faucets or watering troughs. To these spots anyone may come to fill his pail, goatskin, or water cart.

One of the gates into the old city of Fez. (United Nations)

Fez is sometimes referred to as the center of Moroccan thinking, because it has so many schools. Among these is Karouine University, more than one thousand years old and famed throughout the Moslem world. The city contains many lovely palaces and graceful monuments, as well as hotels for tourists who come to visit the *souks* and other attractions.

One of the best-known palaces in the *medina* was built near the close of the last century by a high official, the Grand Vizier Jamai, chief adviser to the sultan. This building is now used as a hotel, the Palais Jamais, operated by the government. To enter the hotel, guests pass through a gate in the city wall, cross a hot and dusty courtyard, and after going down several flights of shaded stone steps, emerge into a cool garden where banana trees, bougainvillea vines, and other flowering tropical plants flourish amid the murmur of fountains.

A lavishly decorated suite of rooms in this hotel contains the former bedroom of the Grand Vizier and those of his various wives, and has a window shaped like a Moorish arch. Through this large window there is a fine view of the city.

Rabat, the City of the King

King Hassan II of Morocco has palaces in several cities, but his headquarters is in Rabat, at the mouth of a river emptying on the Atlantic coast. Rabat has been the capital of Morocco only since 1913, when Moulay Youssef, or the Sultan Joseph, moved his court there from Fez. Because that ancient capital was overrun with

A corner in the garden of the Palais Jamai, now used as a hotel. The elaborate stone carvings behind the banana tree are typical of the delicate ornamentation so important in Moorish architecture. (George R. Harrison)

The changing of the king's palace guard at the capital city of Rabat. (George R. Harrison)

political intrigue, the entire seat of government was moved to Rabat, then a small town, but now grown to the third largest city in Morocco. Only Casablanca and Marrakesh are larger.

The main palace of the king is a low modern building that does not look much like a palace from the outside, but is beautiful within. The changing of the guard in the street in front of the palace grounds is an event always enjoyed by onlookers. Many government offices are connected with the king's residence, and a block away stands a modern army building that houses the general staff.

When King Hassan goes to the mosque on Friday he dresses completely in white, and often rides in a coach given to his great-grandfather by Queen Victoria. So that the people lining the streets can get another view of him, he usually rides back to his palace on a white charger. The king, modern as he is in much of his thinking, still carefully observes the traditional ways of the Moslem religion.

Modern Rabat has broad streets lined with flowers that seem always to be in bloom. The city has many public squares, and buildings for government and business. Its *medina* is very old, and Berbers are known to have lived there as far back as A.D. 790. This *medina* is surrounded by the ancient walls so common in Morocco, while its *casbah*, started in A.D. 1150, is an imposing fortress. Storks' nests line its walls; the birds winter here and fly north in summer to Holland and other parts of Europe.

An outstanding sight in Rabat is the Tour Hassan, or Hassan's Tower, a building that was begun in the middle of the twelfth

Hassan's Tower, in Rabat. (Huffman—Cushing)

Street scene in Rabat, with posters in French, advertising American motion pictures. (Huffman—Cushing)

century as the minaret of a great mosque. Instead of stairs, the tower has a spiral ramp inside so that horses can be ridden clear to the top. But work on the building was stopped in A.D. 1199, and the tower stands stubby and incomplete. It is still high enough, however, to give a fine view over the sea and the countryside. Its walls, which are 53 feet square at the base and thicker than a man is tall, are 144 feet high — about twelve stories of a modern building. If it had been completed, the tower would have been one of the wonders of its time.

Just across the river from Rabat lies the market town of Salé (sa-LAY). People travel from one place to the other in tiny ferries

— awning-covered rowboats that are pulled across the water by oarsmen. Farther upstream the river is crossed by a modern bridge, used by cars and horses, donkeys and camels. Sometimes sailboat races are held on the river, and the shimmering sails make a lovely sight against the ancient walls of the *medina*.

Cities and Towns of the Western Coast

Of the five largest Moroccan cities, all but Fez and Marrakesh are on the Atlantic coast. Rabat is 140 miles south of Tangier, and 55 miles farther on is the largest city of the country, Casablanca.

View of Casablanca. (United Nations)

The name is Spanish, and means "white house." It is an appropriate name, as most of the city's houses and public buildings are coated with white plaster.

Casablanca has become the busiest city of Morocco, for through its port goes most of the shipping to and from the outside world. In the harbor two long piers protected with jetties have been built far out into the Atlantic. Here freighters dock when they bring goods to be sent overland, and here they load up with Moroccan products.

Casablanca is a thoroughly modern city. Large businesses were established here by the French during their occupation of the country, which lasted from 1912 to 1956. The American Army had headquarters in Casablanca during World War II. The second language of most educated Moroccans is French, except around Tangier, where Spanish is more widely spoken.

Going southward along the Atlantic coast from Casablanca, a traveler passes through several towns built around factories that process phosphate fertilizer or pack fish in cans. Then comes Essaouira (Es-sah-WEE-rah), whose name comes from Arabic words meaning "a small fortress." For several centuries, until a few years ago, the town was known by its Portuguese name of Mogador, which means "safe anchorage." Essaouira has a protected harbor that serves as a port for fishing boats. Most of the fishermen are of Portuguese descent.

This harbor has been used for thousands of years. The Phoenicians are known to have sailed this far south, and the ancient Romans came frequently to obtain a brilliant coloring material produced from shellfish, which they used for dyeing their robes purple. Lining the main street of the town and facing the sea, ancient cannons still stand.

Two old cannons point out to sea at Essaouira, on the Atlantic coast. (George R. Harrison)

A hundred miles south of Essaouira lies Agadir (ag-a-DEER), which in 1960 was completely destroyed by an earthquake. The town has now been rebuilt near its former location, and beyond its harbor, which contains large docks for shipping, stands a big fertilizer factory.

Agadir, like Essaouira, has miles of sandy beach, which attracts many tourists. But the Arab and Berber people who live along the coast do not take naturally to the sea, and show little interest in fishing, although they do gather seaweed on the shore to fertilize their crops.

South of Agadir the desert approaches the sea, and there are few towns on the coast. Below the town of Tiznit lies the small area called Ifni, which still belongs to Spain. Next comes the inland town of Goulimine (GOO-li-MEEN), and beyond that is the Sahara Desert.

People sometimes return from a visit to Morocco with the story that goats there climb trees. This sounds like a fairy tale, but it is true. Many valleys near the southern coast are dotted with wild argan trees, not found anywhere else in the world. These trees are covered with green leaves, even in the dry heat of summer. The trees have low-spreading limbs and bear a small fruit that looks like an olive. Foraging for food, the herdsmen's goats jump into the low branches and climb high into the trees, nibbling away at leaves and fruit as they go. As many as ten goats have been counted in one tree at the same time. The surefooted little creatures venture far out on the branches as they stretch for the tenderest morsels, until it seems as if the limbs will no longer be able to support them. But just in time the little creatures draw back and seek another branch on which to venture.

Near the argan trees the fruit seeds lie scattered on the ground. These are gathered up by the Moroccans and are washed and cracked. From the inner nut is pressed a flavorful, fragrant oil that is used for cooking.

Marrakesh, Gateway to the South

Marrakesh is the most African city of Morocco. Early European writers knew the settlement as Maroc, and this is what the country of Morocco is called today in French.

Marrakesh has a special charm of its own. It lies in the foothills of the High Atlas Mountains, due south of Casablanca and about 100 miles inland from Essaouira on the Atlantic Ocean. The region around Marrakesh is normally dry, but near the city, water has been piped down from reservoirs made by damming streams in the mountains nearby. Orchards of olive trees, and of date palms bearing heavy bunches of fruit high in the air, stretch for miles around

Marrakesh. Many of the streets are lined with orange trees, and gardens are filled with bougainvillea and with flowering jasmine, which gives off a sweet odor after dark.

Marrakesh is famous for its climate. The air is dry and the weather is usually sunny. Seldom too warm or too cold, the region has in recent years become a favorite winter vacation spot for Europeans.

Marrakesh was founded in the eleventh century and at times has been the capital of the region. Among its medieval palaces and other monuments the most famous building is a great tower called the Koutoubiya, a high minaret of sandstone whose top is decorated with tiles of emerald green. (See picture on page 18.)

The large *medina* is surrounded by a wall that is rosy pink in color and contrasts pleasantly with the green foliage of gardens and orchards. This *medina,* more than nine hundred years old, has the usual narrow alleys lined with *souks* where almost anything can be bought, from old bottle caps and dead flashlight batteries to long, coatlike silk garments called caftans (KAF-tanz).

In the *medina* lies a great square called the Djemaa-el-Fna, where in the late afternoon, beginning about four and lasting until dark, thousands of people gather to be entertained. They listen to storytellers; watch snake charmers, magicians, jugglers, or acrobats; hear preachers; and see medicine men demonstrate the miraculous cures in their bottles. This fair, attracting its customers from the nearby *souks,* goes on every day. In the square many cooks tend their braziers while they grill fish or pieces of mutton so that people from the country can have a bite of supper before leaving.

Inside the city the little taxis that go scurrying about are not the only means of transportation. Hundreds of horse-drawn buggies are lined up along the *medina* wall waiting for customers. Near

At the afternoon fair in Marrakesh a snake charmer keeps a wary eye on his reptile. (George R. Harrison)

the *souks* are racks in which are parked hundreds of bicycles, faster on modern roads than the old-time burros and camels, although incapable of carrying such bulky loads.

Many more camels can be seen in Marrakesh than farther north. Each Thursday morning a camel market is held in a field outside the city. There one can buy a little animal just old enough to leave its mother, or a string of ancient desert wanderers ready to set off on a caravan route that may lead as far as Timbuktu.

But not all of Marrakesh is ancient. Starting in 1913, a modern city was built about a mile and a half from the old one. Under the French administration, modern agricultural and commercial training schools were established. The ancient arts and crafts were revived, and their development has been encouraged. Among the manufactures are leather goods and carpets. Other industries are flour milling, wool spinning, and fruit processing. Copper, lead, and graphite are mined in the mountains nearby.

Thirty miles to the south of Marrakesh are two famous passes crossing the High Atlas. Through them wind roads that lead down to southern Morocco and the Sahara. One road leads to the sea at Agadir, then cuts down the coast to Goulimine, from which camel caravans take off into the desert. The other route, after following the road of the *casbahs* for a hundred miles, leads inland to a second entrance to the desert at Zagora. Another branch goes still farther east, meeting trails that run south from the mountains.

A street in the modern section of Marrakesh. (Huffman—Cushing)

The casbah of Telouet in the High Atlas Mountains. (Bertrand, Marrakesh)

CHIEFTAINS OF THE MOUNTAIN TRIBES

One of the most famous *casbahs* in Morocco is that at Telouet, which stands in a valley near the top of the High Atlas Mountains, not more than sixty miles south of Marrakesh. This rambling old pile was built by the Glaoui family, whose chiefs were high officials under the sultan in the early days of this century. One of these leaders, El Glaoui, became pasha of Marrakesh and was instrumental in putting a sultan on the throne during one of the Moroccan wars.

Great numbers of camel caravans carrying hides, wool, rugs, dates, and young animals formerly crossed the High Atlas to Marrakesh and returned with grain, salt, cloth, and other needed materials. Most of the mountain people have tried to make a living by farming, making charcoal, raising goats, or hunting wild boar, and by serving their local chieftain as fighters. But they have always been poor. By keeping control of a mountain pass a chieftain could hope to help support his people by exacting tribute from travelers. But he needed a fortress, or *casbah*, to serve as a base.

The *casbah* at Telouet, which is said to contain more than six hundred rooms, was never finished; work on it was stopped about forty years ago when the owner died. Now, except for a few government guards, it is empty and has fallen into disrepair. Deep underneath the vast pile of walls and battlements made of stones and mud bricks coated with flaking pink plaster are dungeons where prisoners were formerly kept. Many of the upper rooms are beautifully decorated with tiles and mosaics and with stone and wood carved in the Moorish manner.

In the Rif, far to the northeast, lived local chiefs who in the past sometimes swept down to plunder the cities of Tetuán (te-TWAN) and Fez. Many of these tribal rulers were cruel, proud, and fond of fighting. After galloping down on a village in the plain and sacking it, they would ride swiftly back to their mountain strongholds, where they were hard to pursue. The last of the chieftains of the Rif tribes was Abd-el-Krim, a well-educated man whose name means "servant of the Generous." ("The Generous" is one of the ninety-nine names used in the Koran to describe Allah.) In the tribes under him this fierce warrior had thousands of fighters who, in a guerrilla war against the Spanish military government then ruling the area, held out for two years before they were finally defeated in 1926 by twenty times as many French and Spanish soldiers.

Another noted Rif chieftain was named Raisuli. He sought money through kidnapping and ransom. About sixty-five years ago, he abducted an American citizen named Ion Perdicaris. President Theodore Roosevelt of the United States sent the sultan of Morocco a message that read, "Perdicaris alive or Raisuli dead." The sultan induced Raisuli to turn Perdicaris loose, and Raisuli lived to help Abd-el-Krim fight against the Spanish in the 1920's.

An encampment of Bedouins, nomad herdsmen. Their tents are surrounded by walls of thornbushes. (George R. Harrison)

THE BEDOUINS AND THE BLUE PEOPLE

Frequently seen in the dry regions that ring the desert are members of Bedouin tribes — nomads who drive their flocks from place to place in search of pasture. By wandering miles in a day, their goats, sheep, and camels are able to find sustenance on rocky plains and hillsides where a human eye can see scarcely a blade of grass or a weed.

To follow their flocks conveniently, the Bedouins live in large tents, usually woven of black goats' hair. These tents, held up by light wooden poles, can be taken down quickly, packed on the backs of camels, and moved to a new location.

When a group of Bedouins make camp in a place where they expect to stay for more than a few days, they often surround their tents with fences made by piling up dry bushes that have sharp spikes as long as a man's little finger. Such a thorn wall is difficult for robbers to break through, for the spines are like needlepoints. The desert nomads also build thorn corrals to keep their animals from wandering away at night.

The Bedouins always pitch their tents so that they open in a direction that will give protection from wind and sand. The tent floor is covered with rugs, which can be folded up quickly and packed in bales to be carried by the camels.

Another tribal group is called the Tuaregs (TWAH-regz). During the colder part of the year these people live in tents made by sewing animal skins together. But in warmer weather they build huts made by fastening reeds to wooden frames.

The Tuaregs are descended from one of the oldest Berber tribes, which roamed the Sahara for more than a thousand years. They ride camels, and in earlier years made a living by attacking desert caravans. The Tuareg men were very fierce, and carried lances, swords, and heavy leather shields. When they swept in and conquered a tribe living peacefully in an oasis, they were likely to keep its members as vassals and make them pay a tribute of large portions of the crops they raised.

Like other desert nomads, the Tuareg men originally used a veil to protect their faces from sun and sand. Eventually they came to believe that evil spirits might enter their noses or mouths if they unveiled before a stranger. Many of them still wear their veils almost continuously. While eating, they hold the veil away from their face with their left hand.

One branch of the Tuaregs has now become known as the Blue People. About four centuries ago, an English merchant came by ship to Agadir and sold the natives a large quantity of calico cloth that had been dyed a deep indigo blue. In those days not many bright-colored dyes were available, and the brilliant blue appealed to the desert Berbers, who lived amid sand and rocks in a landscape mostly brown or gray or yellow. The Berbers used the cloth for their robes.

Today most of the Blue People are traders. These Tuareg men still wear robes and turbans dyed indigo, and the women wear blue veils. The perspiration produced by the desert heat makes the color run from the dyed cloth, and this stains the wearers' skin bluish. In towns such as Tiznit in the country of the Blue People, even the doors and trim of the houses are painted their favorite color.

LOOKING TO THE FUTURE

Despite its past years of turmoil, Morocco is called by its inhabitants the Fortunate Kingdom, and its symbol is a five-pointed star. The Moroccan flag contains this star outlined in its center in green, on a red background.

Three of Morocco's greatest problems are poverty, disease, and lack of education. The nation is governed by a small, well-to-do, well-educated group, while most of the people are terribly poor. Disease is all too apparent. Many people beg for a living. And on the outskirts of most large cities are hovels put together from canvas, sheets of iron, and packing cases — the homes of the poor.

Since Morocco has great potential wealth, the living conditions of the great mass of the people can be improved. When more of the water that falls as rain and snow in the mountains can be dammed to give electric power, and when the water can be led by canals and flumes to irrigate more of the fertile land that is now so dry, the lot of the people should be better. How quickly progress can be made depends on how well the government is able to organize and direct new projects in public welfare and to raise the money to pay for them. There has been a start, and loans from foreign countries are helping.

One of the principal sources of money at present is the tourist trade. Travelers are attracted to the country's spectacular beauty and to the picturesque traditional ways of living that still survive in this modern age. Morocco can be reached easily by steamship to the ports of Tangier or Casablanca, or by international airlines that fly to Rabat, Casablanca, Tangier, and Marrakesh. The major cities are connected by railroad, and the country is covered by a network of good roads over which modern buses travel. At present, the tourist business brings in about $75 million a year, but the government has begun a drive to increase this income. A goal of building accommodations for thirty thousand more tourists has been set. Private investment by foreign hotel chains is paying part of the cost.

Morocco is an ancient kingdom set among the many new republics of Africa. It is fortunate in having a king who is forward-looking and dedicated to the improvement of his country. Only in recent times have nationwide elections been held, and it was not until 1963 that a national legislature was set up and a prime minister provided for. But the king still has the final say in the making, enforcing, and interpreting of laws. Even though the legislature may pass a law, he may veto it if it is unacceptable to him.

The people's part in governing themselves is just beginning, and they need an improved educational system if they are to govern properly. In a country where large numbers of the inhabitants cannot even read and write and are not familiar with what is going on outside their own village it is difficult for them to vote intelligently on a national level. Many families are so poor and have such trouble in getting enough to eat that their children are sent to work instead of to school. Almost three-quarters of the people of Morocco are farmers or livestock raisers, and many are suspicious of modern methods and cling to the age-old ways of doing things.

Many Moroccan women still keep to their traditional place out of the public view although, as a result of recent reforms, women can vote and can run for public office. Some of them have even been candidates in elections. But they are slow to take their place in civic affairs. Until recently, girls were not sent to school at all, for it was not thought necessary that women should know how to read and write. This situation is gradually being improved.

A modern school in Tetuán, near the Mediterranean coast. (George R. Harrison)

Only a few years ago, fewer than ten boys in a hundred could go to school. In 1958, seven hundred new schoolrooms were built in Morocco, and more have been constructed since. A compulsory primary education program was started in 1964.

Besides improved education, Morocco needs more factories and other ways of providing jobs for the many people who are unemployed. Government projects have helped. Agricultural training centers are teaching farmers new crop methods. A large American ranch has joined with the Moroccan government in establishing a modern livestock-breeding center. Efforts have been made to use present-day production methods in the handicrafts field, without sacrificing the quality of handmade products. Some years ago, a national promotion program enrolled ten thousand young men to build a road through the Rif. Throughout hilly parts of north-central Morocco, many small mountains have been terraced by labor battalions, and thousands of eucalyptus trees have been planted. Originally native to Australia, these trees can grow in a dry climate and will produce firewood and timber in only a few years. A government five-year plan aims at advancing Morocco in many ways.

Experts from the United Nations staff consider plans for terracing the land in the background, on the bank of the Sebou River, near Fez. (United Nations)

Because of the growing demand for highly specialized technicians, United Nations experts helped to plan the training of civil air personnel in Morocco. Here students are seen learning plane maintenance. (United Nations)

Labor unions are fairly strong in Morocco, and these have cooperated with the government in building better homes for poor people. The government has set up public health centers, but the greater number of people still get little medical care.

Morocco has a long way to go in providing employment, education, and a decent standard of living for the majority of its citizens. But the Moroccans are becoming a forward-looking people, and as they learn modern methods of doing things their ancient and beautiful country may be destined to have a bright future.

INDEX

FISK UNIVERSITY LIBRARY